Sheryl Webster
and Finger Industries Ltd present

Meet Sam

Zip

Zap

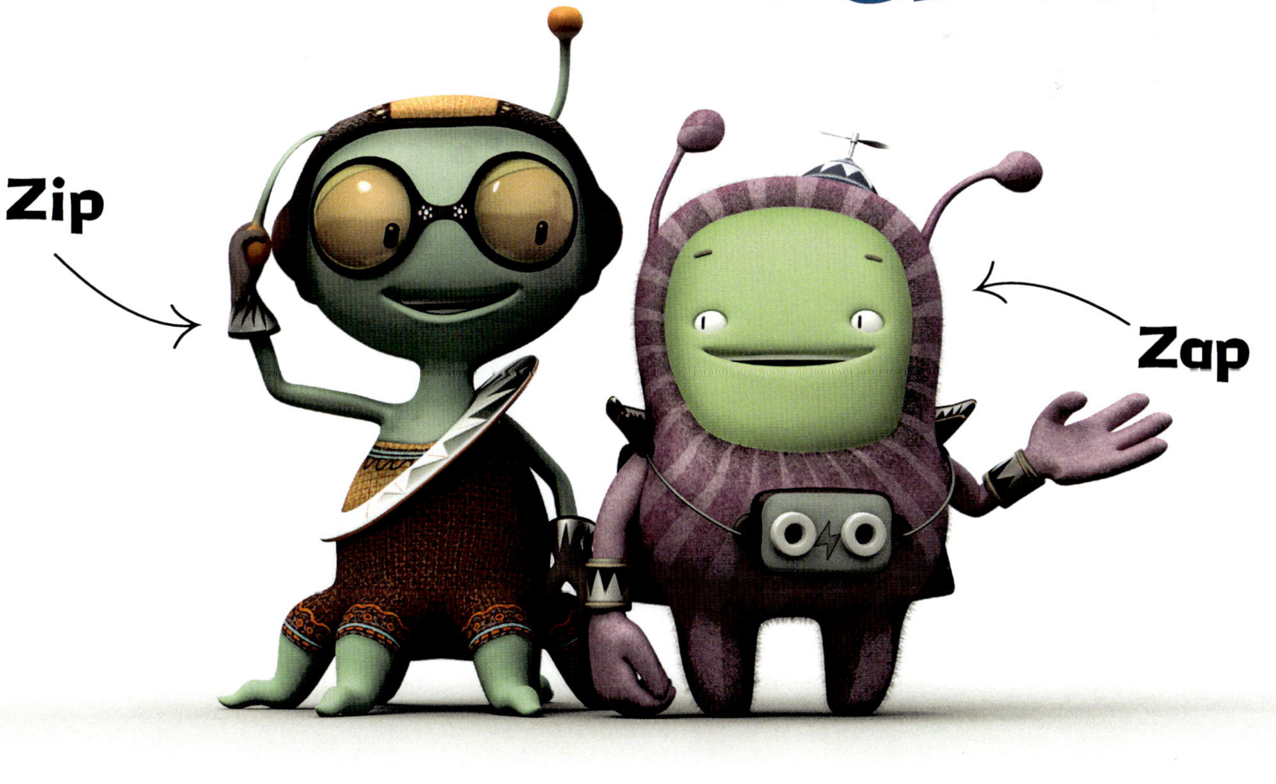

Zip and Zap went on a trip.
They went past the moon.

"What is that?" said Zip.

"I like Sam and Liz," said Zap.
"Me too," said Zip.

“They do not look like us,” said Zap.

"We like to jump in the snow," said Liz.

"We can do that too," said Zip.

"We like to go fast," said Sam.

"We can go fast too," said Zap.

“We have to go,”
said Sam and Liz.

"I will miss Sam and Liz,"
said Zap.

“There is a Sam,”
said Zip.

"Sam can come home with us," said Zap.

"Sam is not here!" said Zap.
"He did not like us!" said Zip.

Look!
Yippee!

"They **do** like us!" said Zip.
"Goodbye Sam and Liz!"
said Zap.